Tomb of the Unknowns

Written by Julia Hargrove

Illustrated by Gary Mohrman

Teaching & Learning Company

1204 Buchanan St., P.O. Box 10
Carthage, IL 62321-0010

This book belongs to

_____

We would like to thank Tom Mani of the U.S. Army Military District of Washington, D.C., Public Affairs Office for his time and effort in checking facts associated with the Tomb of the Unknowns.

Cover photo by Tom Mani courtesy of the U.S. Army Military District of Washington.

Copyright © 2003, Teaching & Learning Company

ISBN No. 1-57310-405-1

Printing No. 987654321

Teaching & Learning Company
1204 Buchanan St., P.O. Box 10
Carthage, IL 62321-0010

Table of Contents

Dear Teacher or Parent,

Welcome again to one of the books in the series on Historic Monuments.

It is March 2003 as I write this introduction, and we are living in unsettled times. Our nation has been involved in a war on terrorism since September 11, 2001, and the destruction of the World Trade Towers. We listen to what are almost daily warnings about terrorist attacks and instructions about how to protect our families against chemical or biological weapons. In this era, which is as perilous as any of the wars described in this book, it is fitting that we remember our veterans and the sacrifices they made to keep our nation whole and dedicated to it constitutional freedoms. Our veterans can be models for our own behavior in a crisis. They can serve as reassurance that we have gotten through difficult situations before and that we will *do* so again. We can take pride in the fact that in our lifetimes we are being tested just as previous generations were tested, and we can resolve that we will successfully meet the test as our predecessors did.

I hope that you find this book to be inspirational as well as educational.

Sincerely,

Julia

Julia Hargrove

Tomb of the Unknowns

The Tomb of the Unknowns is also called the Tomb of the Unknown Soldier.[1] The memorial was first meant to honor an unknown U.S. warrior after World War I. President Warren G. Harding attended the burial of the first Unknown on November 11, 1921, the second anniversary of Armistice Day (the day the fighting ended in World War I). The memorial is located in Arlington National Cemetery in Virginia and bears the inscription: "Here rests in honored glory an American soldier known but to God."[2] After two more wars—World War II and the Korean War—the nation decided that this monument should honor unknown soldiers from all wars. Every year on Veterans Day, ceremonies are held to honor the Unknowns.

The memorial to the unknown soldiers was constructed of white marble from Marble, Colorado. It is called a sarcophagus, which is a stone coffin with ornamentation on it that is displayed in public as a memorial. The carving on the front of the Tomb of the Unknowns shows three Greek figures that stand for peace, victory and valor (or bravery). The white marble sarcophagus was placed directly on top of the grave of the Unknown from World War I. Successive graves of soldiers from World War II, the Korean War and the Vietnam War are to the west of the original monument. Each grave is covered with a white marble slab that is flush with the pavement of the plaza of the Memorial Amphitheater.

U.S. Army Sgt. Edward F. Younger, who had been awarded the Distinguished Service Medal in The Great War, chose the body of the first Unknown. ("The Great War" is what World War I was called before World War II occurred and the wars began to be numbered.) Four bodies from four U.S. cemeteries in France were dug up and laid in identical caskets in the city hall in Chalons-sur-Marne, France, on October 24, 1921. Sgt. Younger chose at random the third casket from the left and designated his choice by laying a spray of white roses on the coffin. The U.S.S. *Olympia* returned the casket to the United States, where the Unknown Soldier lay in state in the Capitol Rotunda until Armistice Day. President Harding presided over the reburial of the Unknown on November 11, 1921.

President Eisenhower signed a congressional bill on August 3, 1956, that provided for the selection and reburial of a soldier from World War II and one from the Korean War. For the choice of the World War II soldier, bodies were brought from burial sites in Europe, Africa, Hawaii and the Philippines. From among these soldiers, two were chosen: one from the European theater and one from the Pacific theater. The bodies were taken aboard the U.S.S. *Canberra* where Congressional Medal of Honor winner Navy Hospitalman 1st Class William R. Charette chose between the two bodies. The one not chosen was buried at sea with appropriate ceremonies.

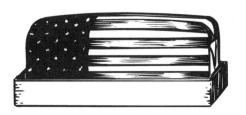

---

[1]"Tomb of the Unknown Soldier": http://www.mdw.army.mil/FS-A04.htm
[2]*The Family Encyclopedia of American History*, Pleasantville, New York, The Reader's Digest Association, Inc., 1975.

Tomb of the Unknowns

At the same time the Unknown Soldier was chosen for World War II, the same process was going on for a Korean War soldier. Four caskets containing unknown soldiers from that war were dug up from the National Cemetery of the Pacific in Hawaii. Army Master Sgt. Ned Lyle chose the casket to be reburied at the Tomb of the Unknowns. The bodies of the veterans of the two wars lay in state in the Capitol Rotunda from May 28 to May 30, 1958. On Memorial Day (May 30), President Eisenhower awarded both soldiers the Medal of Honor. The two were then reburied next to the marble memorial where the Unknown Soldier from World War I was honored.

Although U.S. troops officially left Vietnam in 1973 and the war ended in 1975, it wasn't until 1984 that an Unknown from that war was chosen. Medal of Honor winner U.S. Marine Corps Sgt. Maj. Allan Jay Kellogg, Jr., selected the body in a ceremony at Pearl Harbor, Hawaii, on May 17, 1984. The body of this Unknown also lay in state in the U.S. Capitol Rotunda. President Ronald Reagan officiated at the Memorial Day ceremonies at Arlington National Cemetery where reburial beside the Tomb of the Unknowns occurred. In 1998, the remains of the Vietnam Unknown were identified through DNA testing as Air Force 1st Lt. Michael Joseph Blassie. Blassie's family had pushed to have the remains tested, and when they were identified, they had their hero moved to Jefferson Barracks National Cemetery, near the family home in St. Louis, Missouri, July 11, 1998. The crypt has remained vacant, but was dedicated on POW/MIA Day in 1999 to the missing servicemembers of all wars, with the inscription: "Honoring and Keeping Faith with America's Missing Servicemen." POW-MIA Day is celebrated the third Friday of every September.

Name_____

Tomb of the Unknowns Questions

1. The memorial to an unknown soldier was originally built to honor a warrior from which war?

   _____

2. Write a general description of the way in which each Unknown Soldier was chosen for burial at the

   national monument. _____

   _____

   _____

3. Research Question: What title does the President of the U.S. hold relative to the military that makes it appropriate for him to preside over the burial services at the Tomb of the Unknowns? (Hint: Look

   in Article II of the Constitution.) _____

   _____

   _____

4. Why were two soldiers chosen for burial at the Tomb of the Unknowns in 1958? _____

   _____

   _____

5. Why is there no soldier from the Vietnam War buried at the Tomb of the Unknowns?

   _____

   _____

6. Thought Question: If we have been in a war against terrorism since 9/11/01, shouldn't an unknown victim of the collapse of the World Trade Towers be buried at the Tomb of the Unknowns? Support

   your answer with logical arguments. _____

   _____

   _____

Arlington National Cemetery[1]

Arlington National Cemetery in Virginia is the site of the Tomb of the Unknowns. The cemetery has a fine pedigree, having belonged to George Washington, the first President of the United States, and Mary Anna Lee, the wife of Civil War General Robert E. Lee. From George Washington, the land passed to his adopted grandson, George Washington Parke Custis, a descendent of Martha Washington by her first husband. Custis's only child, Mary Anna Randolph Custis, married her childhood friend and distant cousin, Robert E. Lee. Lee became the custodian of Arlington through his wife's estate.

When Virginia seceded from the Union in 1861, Lee became a Major General in the Confederate Army. Lee feared then that the Union would take over his wife's land and house because the property was just outside Washington, D.C. Federal troops under Brigadier General Irvin McDowell surrounded the 1100 acres of Arlington shortly after Virginia seceded and built two forts on the outskirts of the estate. The federal government took over the land and house when Mrs. Lee did not appear in person to pay property taxes on Arlington. A tax commissioner bought the estate at public auction in January 1864. On June 15, 1864, Brigadier General Montgomery C. Meigs took over the land for a military cemetery.

Neither Robert E. Lee nor his wife Mary Anna tried publicly to have Arlington returned to them after the Civil War. In 1870, their oldest son, George Washington Custis Lee, took his case to the Circuit Court of Virginia claiming that the land had been illegally taken.

According to his grandfather's will, Arlington should belong to Lee. A Supreme Court decision in 1882 returned the land to Lee by a 5-4 decision. In March 1883, the federal government bought the land from Lee for $150,000. The property became a military reservation.

One of the first monuments built in Arlington was a burial vault containing the remains of 1800 men who died at Bull Run and other Virginia battlesites. Veterans of the Revolutionary War, World War II and the Persian Gulf War are also buried there. President John F. Kennedy's grave, topped by an eternal flame, is in Arlington. The last resting places of three Chief Justices and eight Associate Justices of the Supreme Court—including the first African American appointee, Thurgood Marshall—are here. African American Congressional Medal of Honor winners, Japanese-American servicemen from World War II, various astronauts and some important women in U.S. history are also buried at Arlington National Cemetery.[2]

Sentinels from the 3rd U.S. Infantry (The Old Guard) protect the Tomb of the Unknowns continually. All of the sentinels are volunteers, and they must meet difficult physical and mental requirements in order to become guards of the Unknown Soldiers. Only 400 have earned Tomb Guard Badges since 1958. The impressive changing of the guard ceremony occurs every hour from October 1 through March 31 and every half hour between April 1 and September 30. The guards at the Tomb walk in a pattern of 21 steps and 21-second pauses to symbolize the 21-gun salute that is the highest of military honors.

---

[1]"Historical Information": www.arlingtoncemetery.org/historical_information/arlington_house.html

[2]"Ceremonies": www.arlingtoncemetery.org/historical_information/index.html

Arlington National Cemetery Questions

1. Draw a simple genealogical chart to demonstrate the way Arlington passed from George Washington.

2. a. How did the federal government first get ownership of Arlington? b. How did the U.S. government

   get the land back in 1883? _____

   _____

   _____

   _____

3. List four groups of famous people whose graves are at Arlington National Cemetery.

   _____

   _____

4. Why is it appropriate that the sentinels at the Tomb of the Unknowns should have to meet such high

   physical and mental standards? _____

   _____

5. Thought Question: Why are most U.S. Presidents not buried at Arlington National Cemetery?

   _____

   _____

World War I[1]

World War I—which involved troops from four continents, cost the lives of nearly seven million soldiers, ended four empires and dethroned four ruling dynasties—was set off by the death of one man. What single man could be so important that his death would cause a world war? He was Archduke Francis Ferdinand, the heir to the Austro-Hungarian throne; and Austria-Hungary was one of most important empires in Europe. When Gavrilo Princeps assassinated the archduke in the cause of Serbian independence from the Austro-Hungarian Empire, he set off a chain of events that seemed unstoppable and changed the world forever.

The links in the unstoppable chain were the members of two opposing alliances: the Triple Alliance and the Triple Entente. Russia, France and Great Britain were members of the Triple Entente who had pledged to support each other if any one of them was attacked. The members of the Triple Alliance—Germany, Austria and Italy—had a similar agreement. When Russia backed her fellow Slavs in Serbia against Austria-Hungary, the Germans offered Austria unconditional support. Then Russia mobilized its troops and sent them to the Russian border with Germany. Germany was caught between Russia on its eastern border and Russia's ally, France, on its western border. Germany struck first by invading France through neutral Belgium. The attack on Belgium and France brought Great Britain into the war. Suddenly, all of Europe was in flames!

Now it was the Central Powers versus the Allied Powers. The Central Powers were Germany, Austria-Hungary and Italy—in the center of Europe—and later Turkey and Bulgaria. The Allied Powers consisted of France, Great Britain, Russia and later Japan. Italy changed sides in 1915 after being conquered by the Allies. The United States declared war on the Central Powers in 1917 and joined the fighting on the side of the Allies. The Communist Revolution in November 1917 brought V.I. Lenin to power in Russia. Lenin took Russia out of the war in March 1918.[2]

The United States stayed out of World War I as long as it could. When President Woodrow Wilson ran for re-election in 1916, his slogan was: "He kept us out of war." However, the issue of Germany's unrestricted submarine warfare eventually drew the U.S. into the fighting. The sinking of the *Lusitania* by a German submarine in May 1915 with the loss of 1198 lives, including 128 Americans, is just one example of the reasons the U.S. went to war.

---

[1]*The American Pageant* (7th ed.) by Thomas A. Bailey and David M. Kennedy, Lexington, Massachusetts, D.C. Heath and Company, 1983.

[2]*World History: Patterns of Civilization* by Burton F. Beers, Englewood Cliffs, New Jersey, Prentice-Hall, Inc., 1984.

World War I

I WANT YOU FOR U. S. ARMY

NEAREST RECRUITING STATION

Although the United States declared war against the Central Powers in April 1917, it wasn't until nearly seven months later, on October 23, 1917, that U.S. troops saw their first fighting in Europe. Americans fought in seven major areas of France: Ypres, Cantigny, Soissons, Belleau Wood, Chateau-Thierry, the Meuse-Argonne and St. Mihiel. At Chateau-Thierry and Belleau Wood, U.S. troops helped stop the last great German push against Paris. The American Marines were so heroic at Belleau Wood that the French renamed the area "Bois de Marins" or Marine Woods. American soldiers who fought in the Second Battle of the Marne helped drive back German troops in a reversal that eventually ended the war. The Meuse-Argonne offensive from September 26, 1918, to November 11, 1918, involved 1,200,000 U.S. soldiers. The U.S. suffered 10 percent casualties during those weeks, with 120,000 men killed or wounded. With the help of the Americans, the Allies were defeating the Central Powers. By October 1918, the Germans were ready to surrender to the Allies. An armistice, or an agreed end to the fighting, occurred at 11 a.m. on 11-11-1918.

November 11 was celebrated each year as Armistice Day beginning in 1919. In 1954, the holiday was renamed Veterans Day so that November 11 would be a day to honor veterans of World War II and the Korean War as well as those of World War I. Although Veterans Day briefly became one of the Monday holidays (1971-1975), many people still hold parades and memorial services on November 11 in honor of the original Armistice Day and Veterans Day.[3]

---

[3]*The Family Encyclopedia of American History*, Pleasantville, New York, The Reader's Digest Association, Inc., 1975.

Name_____

World War I Questions

1. What event was the immediate cause of World War I? _____

_____

2. Explain how the Triple Alliance and the Triple Entente drew almost all of Europe into the war.

_____

_____

3. Mark two columns on the back of this sheet. In the left-hand column, make a chart showing the members of the Allied Powers in 1914 and, below that, the members of the Central Powers in 1914. In the the right-hand column, show the members of the Allied Powers in 1918 and, below that, the members of the Central Powers in 1918. This will show how the members of each alliance changed during the war.

4. a. What problem with Germany eventually drew the United States into the war against the Central

   Powers? b. Give a specific example of Germany's actions that caused this problem. _____

_____

_____

5. How long did it take after the declaration of war for the U.S. to train its troops, transport them to

   Europe and engage them in the fighting there? _____

6. In what seven major areas did U.S. troops fight in France? _____

_____

_____

7. What was the result of U.S. troops' fighting at Belleau Wood and Chateau-Thierry?

_____

_____

8. Explain why November 11 was celebrated as Veterans Day.

_____

_____

TLC10405 Copyright © Teaching & Learning Company, Carthage, IL 62321-001

Name_____

General Pershing & the World War I Monuments[1]

General John Pershing was a man of war who led the American Expeditionary Force into battle in France during World War I. He was also a man of peace who planned several cemeteries and monuments to be built in France with sensitivity both to the honor of the dead and the pride of the French.

Eighty thousand U.S. soldiers died in France in 1917-1918, the time the U.S. fought in World War I. Although the families of many soldiers preferred that their loved ones be brought home for burial, the bodies of about 31,000 servicemen remained in France. Cemeteries created during the war were often crude, dug between the end of one battle and the time the troops had to move on to fight the next. They were often in the middle of farmers' fields whose owners had to plow around the graves. There was no provision for upkeep of these cemeteries, and they became run down and overgrown with weeds. Pershing was determined that the cemeteries be beautiful and fitting places to honor the sacrifices of the dead.

Pershing urged the U.S. government to create a Battle Monuments Board under the authority of the War Department. (The former War Department is now the Department of Defense, a part of the President's Cabinet.) Congress passed a law creating the American Battle Monuments Commission (ABMC) in 1923 and appointed General Pershing to head it.

One of the first decisions the Commission faced was how many monuments should be built in France. Here Pershing showed his sensitivity to France's pride. While the U.S. had lost about 80,000 men, the French had suffered the deaths of one million of their soldiers. It would be tacky for the U.S. to have more monuments or more elaborate monuments than the French did. Once this was decided, the Commission moved to limit the number of memorials to U.S. soldiers by getting the French and Belgian governments to agree that they would allow only the ABMC to create cemeteries and monuments in those two countries.

A year after Congress created the ABMC, its members toured the battlefields of Europe. They decided that the monuments would be constructed near battlefields where Americans actually fought but also close to major population centers or highways to attract tourists. Finally they decided on five minor monuments and three major ones. The five smaller memorials would be located at Sommepy, Cantigny, Kemmel, Audenarde and Bellicourt. The major monuments would be built at Chateau-Thierry (near the Aisne-Marne battlefield), Montsec (near the St. Mihiel battlefield) and at Montfaucon (near the Meuse-Argonne battlefield). The American architects chosen to design the monuments were John Russell Pope for Montfaucon, Egerton Swarwout for Montsec and Paul P. Cret for Chateau-Thierry. The ABMC also wanted a guidebook that accurately described the battlefields. The Commission published the resulting *Guide to the American Battle Fields in Europe* in 1927.

---

[1]"Honoring the Nation's Dead" by Donald Smythe, *American History Illustrated*, Vol. XVI, No. 2, May 1981, pp. 26-33.

General Pershing & the World War I Monuments

Another huge task of the Commission was to rebury the bodies of U.S. soldiers in the new cemeteries with their monuments. Part of the difficulty was in locating the bodies because servicemen had been buried in 2400 places in Europe. The Commission had these remains transferred to eight cemeteries—one in England, one in Belgium and six in France.

The monuments, although all different from each other in design, are similar in their qualities of beauty, dignity and peace. The memorial at Montfaucon stands at the top of a series of flights of stairs. It is a tall column with a statue on top. At Cantigny, the dead are honored by a pillar with only a little ornamentation at the top two levels. People who visit the Montsec monument, see an open rotunda of Greek columns. It looks something like the Jefferson Memorial in Washington, D.C. At Chateau-Thierry, the memorial appears to be an open wall or room with two rows of pillars topped by a stone roof with simple ornamentation. Two statues are carved on one side of the wall. The motto on the Tomb of the Unknowns was first inscribed on the graves of Unknown Soldiers buried at the memorials in France.

The American Battle Monument Commission continues to oversee U.S. cemeteries in foreign lands. Since World War II, more cemeteries have been added to the Commission's responsibilities, including those in the Philippines, Hawaii, Italy and Normandy in France. The Commission maintains 24 permanent U.S. cemeteries overseas.[2]

Montfaucon American Monument

Cantigny American Monument

Montsec American Monument

[2]"ABMC Cemeteries": www.usabmc.com/abmc2.htm

Name_____

General Pershing & the
World War I Monuments Questions

1. Why did General Pershing want to limit the number and size of U.S. monuments in France after

   World War I? _____

   _____

2. What were two reasons that new cemeteries were necessary after the war ended?

   _____

   _____

3. a. How many minor monuments and cemeteries were constructed? b. What were the locations of the

   three major monuments and cemeteries? _____

   _____

   _____

4. Thought Question: What are two reasons why tourists would want to visit the cemeteries and monu-

   ments of soldiers who were killed in wars that happened 60 to 90 years ago? _____

   _____

   _____

Name_____

World War II Time Line[1]

1939

September 1—Germany invades Poland, beginning World War II

September 17—Soviet Union invades Poland from the east

November 30—Soviet troops invade Finland

1940

April 9—German troops invade Denmark and Norway

May10—German troops invade Netherlands, Luxemburg, Belgium and France

May 26-June 4—successful evacuation of French and British troops from Dunkirk, France; 338,226 men saved

July-October—German submarines sink 217 merchant ships in the Atlantic

July 4—Italian troops attack the Sudan

July 25—Soviet Union annexes Latvia, Estonia and Lithuania

August 4-21—Italians occupy British Somaliland

September 7—Germans begin air raids on London, England (the Blitz)

September 11—Italian troops attack Egypt

September 22—Japanese troops invade northern French Indochina (now divided into Thailand, Cambodia, Laos and Vietnam)

October 28—Italian troops invade Greece

1941

February 25—British and American troops recapture Somaliland

March 9—Italians attack Albania, but invasion fails

April 6—Germany invades Yugoslavia and Greece

June 22—Germany attacks Soviet Union

August 20—beginning of German siege of Leningrad in the Soviet Union

December 7—Japanese ships and planes attack Pearl Harbor, Hawaii

December 7-8—Japanese invade Malaya, Hong Kong, Guam, Midway, Wake, the Philippine Islands and Thailand

December 16—Japanese invade Borneo and Burma

---

[1]Dates and events adapted from *The Reader's Digest Illustrated History of World War II*, edited by Michael Wright, London, The Reader's Digest Association Limited, 1989.

World War II Time Line

1942

January 30-31—Germans defeat British at El Alamein, Egypt

March 14—U.S. troops arrive in Australia to begin Pacific counteroffensive

April 5—Japanese troops attack Ceylon (now called Sri Lanka)

April 18—Doolittle leads U.S. bombers in first attack on Tokyo, Japan

May 4-8—Allies win Battle of the Coral Sea in the Pacific Ocean

June 4-8—Allies defeat Japanese in Battle of Midway in Pacific Ocean

June 6-8—Japanese capture Attu and Kiska, Aleutian Islands near Alaska

July 14—Congress Party demands British leave India and grant independence

August 7—U.S. troops land on Guadalcanal in the Solomon Islands

September 13—siege and battle of Stalingrad, Soviet Union, begins

November 8—U.S. and other Allied troops land in Morocco and Algeria

November 11—last German and Italian troops driven out of Egypt

November 12-15—Allies win naval Battle of Guadalcanal

1943

January 27—first U.S. air raids on Germany

February 2—last German troops surrender in Stalingrad, Soviet Union

February 14-25—Germans defeat Allies at Battle of Kasserine Pass, Tunisia

May 13—Axis troops (German and Italian) surrender in North Africa

June 29-30—Australian and U.S. troops land in New Guinea

July 9-10—U.S. troops invade Sicily, an island that is part of Italy

September 3—Italians secretly surrender to the United States, but German troops continue to fight against Allies in Italy

September 9—Allied troops land at Salerno, Italy

November 20-23—U.S. troops capture Tarawa in Gilbert Islands

November 28-30—Big Three (Churchill, Roosevelt, Stalin) meet at Teheran (Iran) Conference

World War II Time Line

1944

January 22—U.S. troops and Allies land at Anzio, Italy

June 4—Allies capture Rome, Italy

June 6—D-Day—the Allied invasion of Normandy coast in France begins

June 15-July 9—Allies capture Saipan in the Mariana Islands

August 25—Allied forces liberate Paris, France

September 8—Germany launches first V-2 rockets on London, Great Britain

October 20—MacArthur lands with U.S. troops on Leyte in the Philippines

December 16—beginning of German counter-attack on Allies in Europe known as the Battle of the Bulge

December 26—General Patton's tanks relieve siege of Allied-held Bastogne, Belgium, in the Battle of the Bulge

1945

January 17-19—Soviets take Warsaw, Cracow, Lodz and Tarnow in Poland

February 19—U.S. Marines invade Iwo Jima Island in Pacific Ocean

February 25—U.S. conducts first fire bombings of Tokyo, Japan

April 1—U.S. troops invade Okinawa

April 7—Allies defeat Japanese navy in Battle of the East China Sea

April 25—U.S. and Soviet troops meet at Torgau, Germany, on the Elbe River

May 2—Germans surrender Italy to Allies; Berlin, Germany, surrenders to Soviets

May 7—Germany surrenders to U.S. and other Allies

May 8—V.E. Day (Victory in Europe); Germans surrender to U.S.S.R.

August 6—U.S drops first atomic bomb on Hiroshima, Japan

August 8—Soviet Union declares war against Japan

August 9—U.S. drops second atomic bomb on Nagasaki, Japan; Soviet army invades Manchuria, China

August 15—V.J. Day (Victory in Japan) as Emperor Hirohito accepts U.S. terms of surrender

August 23—U.S. troops land in Japan to begin occupation of that nation

September 2—treaty of surrender signed by Japanese and Allied officials aboard the battleship *Missouri* in Tokyo Bay

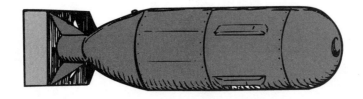

World War II Time Line Activities

1. On the back of this sheet, divide the page into four columns. Label the four columns with the following titles: *German Aggression, Italian Aggression, Japanese Aggression* and *Soviet Aggression.* Then fill in the columns with examples of aggression by each of those nations using events from 1939-1941 only.

2. The year 1942 was the turning of the tide for the Allies as they began to win the war. List all eight events from the year 1942 on the time line that show the Allies are beginning to win the war.

_____

_____

_____

_____

3. The major areas in which fighting occurred during World War II were Europe, the Asian mainland, the Pacific Ocean and its islands and North Africa. On another sheet of paper, divide your page into four columns. The headings on these columns will be the names of the four geographical areas listed in the first sentence of this activity. You will then place each of the events shown for the year 1943 under the correct geographical heading on your chart. Use the maps in your history book in the chapters on World War II to help you.

4. What two nations did the Allies recapture in 1944? (Hint: Capturing the capital of a nation often means the nation is conquered or reclaimed.)_____

_____

_____

5. In the first activity with this time line, the chart shows that the Soviet Union was conquering nations and appeared to be one of the aggressors along with Germany, Italy and Japan. In 1945 on the time line, the Soviet Union is one of the Allies fighting to defeat the Axis Powers, particularly Germany.
   a. Name two events in 1945 that confirm that the Soviet Union was fighting on the side of the Allies.
   b. Name two events in 1941 that explain why the Soviet Union changed sides.

_____

_____

_____

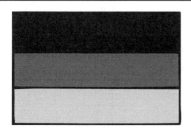 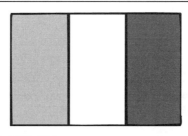 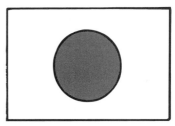

International World War II Cemeteries

Since World War II was fought on four continents, U.S. soldiers are buried all over the world. There are 24 cemeteries under the permanent care of the American Battle Monument Commission. Nearly 125,000 soldiers from World War I and World War II are buried in England, France, Italy, North Africa, the Philippines, Hawaii and other places. The author chose to describe the following four cemeteries because of their locations near major theaters of battle in World War II.

North Africa American Cemetery and Memorial [1]

The United States and its Allies invaded North Africa in November 1942. Allied planners decided it was necessary to clear the Axis Powers from Africa before they could invade Europe. Two thousand eight hundred forty-one Americans are buried on 27 acres near Carthage, Tunisia. Carthage itself is an ancient battle site from the Third Punic War between the Romans and Carthaginians. The Romans destroyed Carthage in 146 B.C.

The cemetery is laid out in nine rectangular plots. Wide paths that divide the plots contain reflecting pools where the paths intersect with each other. A chapel and memorial court lie within the cemetery. The memorial court contains large mosaic and ceramic maps that show the World War II operations in North Africa and the Persian Gulf area. A Wall of the Missing also stands in the cemetery and on it are listed the 3724 Americans whose bodies were never recovered.

Manila American Cemetery and Memorial [2]

Manila is the capital city of the Philippines, which are a group of islands in the Pacific Ocean. The Japanese had taken over many large island groups in the Pacific on December 7-8, 1941. The United States began the fight to retake the islands in August 1942 with an attack on Guadalcanal in the Solomon Islands. The cemetery in Manila is the resting place of the largest number of men who died in World War II; 17,206 soldiers are buried there. They are from the battles on New Guinea and the Philippines.

The Manila American Cemetery is located six miles outside of the city of Manila on what used to be Fort William McKinley when the U.S. owned the Philippines. Today, the Filipinos call the military installation Fort Bonifacio. The cemetery consists of 11 large plots laid out in a roughly circular pattern on 152 acres of land. A chapel lies in the middle of the cemetery. In front of the chapel are two hemicycles (half circles) with rooms at each end. Each room commemorates the men who fought in four Asian theaters: the Pacific, China, India and Burma. Inscribed on limestone piers inside each hemicycle are the names of 36,282 who are Missing in Action and buried in unknown graves throughout Asia.

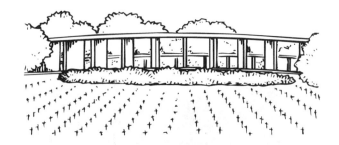

---

[1]"North Africa American Cemetery and Memorial": www.usabmc.com/na.htm

[2]"Manila American Cemetery and Memorial": www.usabmc.com/ml.htm

International World War II Cemeteries

Florence American Cemetery and Memorial [3]

After the U.S. and its Allies had driven Germany and Italy out of North Africa, they began the invasion of Europe. They first attacked Sicily, an island that is part of Italy, in July 1943. Later they fought for a foothold on the Italian mainland at Anzio and Salerno. Most of those buried in the cemetery at Florence were killed in the battle to capture Rome, the capital of Italy, in June 1944, and in the fighting in the Apennine Mountains in April and May 1945.

The 70-acre cemetery is located about seven miles south of Florence. It is west of the Greve River on a sloping hillside. The headstones of 4402 Americans are arranged in curved rows up the hill. The memorial is situated at the top of the cemetery on a broad terrace. Part of the memorial is a tall column with a sculpted figure on top. The Tablets of the Missing with the names of 1409 soldiers carved on them are across the courtyard from the column. The memorial also contains a chapel and a map carved in marble that shows U.S. military operations near Florence.

Normandy American Cemetery and Memorial [4]

D-Day, the invasion of France and the beginning of the push into Germany, was on June 6, 1944. It was the largest amphibious (sea to land) attack ever attempted, with 4000 landing ships; 600 warships; 10,000 airplanes; and 176,000 Allied troops.[5] Operation Overlord (as the invasion was code named) was a success; and 11 months later on May 8, 1945, the Allies celebrated Victory in Europe Day.

The cemetery is located on a cliff above Omaha Beach, which was one of the major landing sites of the Normandy invasion. Nine thousand three hundred eighty-six Americans are buried on its 172-acre site. One thousand five hundred fifty-seven more men who were Missing in Action have their names carved on the walls surrounding a garden on the east side of the memorial. The memorial also contains a chapel, two sets of maps with explanations of the military operations in the area and a statue called "The Spirit of Youth." Behind the chapel are two other statues that symbolize the United States and France.

[3]"Florence American Cemetery and Memorial": www.usabmc.com/fl.htm
[4]"Normandy American Cemetery and Memorial": www.usabmc.com/no.htm
[5]*The Almanac of American History* edited by Arthur M. Schlesinger, Jr., New York, Barnes and Noble Books, 1993, p. 497.

Name_____

International World War II Cemeteries Chart

Fill in the chart below with information from the text on World War II cemeteries. When you reach the part of the chart that lists ele-ments included in the memorial, circle *yes* if it is part of the memorial or circle *no* if it is not part of the memorial.

Questions	North Africa American Cemetery & Memorial	Manila American Cemetery & Memorial	Florence American Cemetery & Memorial	Normandy American Cemetery & Memorial
Continent Where Located	Africa	Asia (Pacific Islands)	Europe	Europe
Located Near What City or Site				
Number of U.S. Dead Buried at the Cemetery				
Number of Missing in Action Listed at Cemetery				
Size of Cemetery (in acres)				
Describe the Major Military Action Associated with the Cemetery				

Memorial Includes Which of the Following?

Chapel	Yes	No	Yes	No	Yes	No	Yes	No
Maps of Operation	Yes	No	Yes	No	Yes	No	Yes	No
Names of Missing Men	Yes	No	Yes	No	Yes	No	Yes	No
Statues	Yes	No	Yes	No	Yes	No	Yes	No
Column/Pillar	Yes	No	Yes	No	Yes	No	Yes	No

Name _____

Korean War[1]

On June 25, 1950, North Korean forces crossed the 38th parallel, the dividing line between North and South Korea. U.S. President Harry S. Truman took the issue of Communist aggression to the United Nations Security Council. The Soviet Union's representative was absent in protest of some other action, so the Security Council was able to vote unanimously to support South Korea. On June 27, Truman sent U.S. Air Force and Navy forces to fight against North Korea. President Truman also sent General Douglas MacArthur and his troops stationed in Japan into battle. Truman did not ask Congress for a declaration of war, which is one reason this war is often called a "conflict" or "police action" instead of a war.

The South Korean troops had been pushed to the bottom of their peninsula and held only a small area around Pusan. General MacArthur decided not to fight back up the peninsula but to surprise the North Koreans by attacking behind their lines. He designed an amphibious (sea to land) operation that would send U.S. troops to Inchon, South Korea, near the 38th parallel and close to the capital city, Seoul. The daring attack occurred on September 15, 1950, and succeeded against all odds. After two more weeks, the North Koreans had retreated into their own country. However, that was not the end of the war.

In the wake of MacArthur's success at Inchon, the South Korean troops had crossed into North Korea chasing the North Koreans. The United Nations General Assembly and President Truman both allowed General MacArthur and his troops to cross the 38th parallel into North Korea as long as they did not provoke a response from either Communist China or the Soviet Union, who were North Korea's allies. In November 1950, as MacArthur approached the Yalu River (the boundary between North Korea and China), thousands of Chinese troops crossed into North Korea and drove the United Nations forces back to the 38th parallel. To fight this new enemy, MacArthur recommended a naval blockade of Chinese ports and the bombing of Chinese bases in Manchuria. However, the U.S. did not want a war with China. As the famous quotation from the Chairman of the Joint Chiefs of Staff, General Omar Bradley, said, a war in Asia would be "the wrong war, at the wrong place, at the wrong time and with the wrong enemy."

General MacArthur resented being restrained in his ability to fight and declared, "There is no substitute for victory." He began to criticize the President's policies. At a ceremony in which Truman awarded MacArthur yet another medal, Truman also talked with the general about his outspokenness. When MacArthur continued to publicly criticize his Commander in Chief, Truman had no alternative but to fire him. On April 11, 1951, MacArthur was removed from his command for insubordination. With the aggressive general gone, the opponents began peace negotiations in July of 1951.

---

[1]*The American Pageant* (7th ed.) by Thomas A. Bailey and David M. Kennedy, Lexington, Massachusetts, D.C. Heath and Company, 1983.

Korean War

The issue of prisoner exchange kept the negotiations dragging on and on. Part of the problem was that the Communists feared that Chinese and North Korean prisoners of war would not want to return to their countries, which would be humiliating proof that life under Communism was not as good as the Communists wanted everyone to believe. With the negotiations going nowhere, the fighting continued. In 1952, Dwight Eisenhower was elected President, and he succeeded Truman in January 1953. "I shall go to Korea," Eisenhower had promised during his campaign; and the former World War II general spent three days in Korea in December 1952 (after his election but before his inauguration).

In spite of Eisenhower's visit to Korea, the war continued for seven more months. The President then threatened to use atomic weapons to end the war, and that finally brought about an armistice (cease-fire) in July 1953. Although Communism has fallen in Eastern Europe and Germany has been reunited, the division between Communist North Korea and democratic South Korea remains today. Violations of the armistice and "incidents" along the border between the two countries continue to occur.

The Korean "police action" took a heavy toll on the United States. Around 54,000 U.S. soldiers died. The cost of the war was tens of billions of dollars. It was the first war that the United States did not win outright. Soon Korea became "the forgotten war." It was not until 1995—after the Vietnam Veterans Memorial was built—that a monument to the veterans of Korea was finally placed on the Mall in Washington, D.C.

Name _____

Korean War Questions

1. What incident began the Korean War? _____

   _____

2. What brilliant move did General MacArthur make to break out of the stalemate at Pusan, South Korea,

   and regain the initiative in the war? _____

   _____

   _____

3. What two nations were allies of North Korea that the U.S. did not want to draw into the war?

   _____

4. a. Explain in simple terms why President Truman fired General MacArthur. b. Thought Question:
   Truman's firing of MacArthur caused a great uproar in the U.S. In your opinion, should MacArthur
   have been fired? Support your answer with historical facts and logic.

   _____

   _____

   _____

5. What is one reason why the Korean War became "the forgotten war"? _____

   _____

6. Historical Research Question: What kind of power does the Soviet Union (and France, the United
   States, Great Britain and China) have in the U.N. Security Council that could have stopped U.N. sup-

   port of South Korea? _____

   _____

   _____

North
Korea

South
Korea

Punchbowl National Cemetery, Hawaii[1]

The Punchbowl, on the island of Oahu in Hawaii, is one of two U.S. national cemeteries in the Pacific Ocean. (The other is the American Military Cemetery near Manila, the capital of the Philippines, and has been described on page 20 in this book under "International World War II Cemeteries.") The national cemetery in Hawaii contains the remains of World War II servicemen, 800 unidentified Korean War dead and veterans of the Vietnam War.

The Punchbowl got its name because of its shape. It lies in the 116-acre crater of an extinct volcano that looks like a large bowl. The volcano was named Pouwaina, which appropriately means "Consecrated Hill" or "Hill of Sacrifice." Historically, the volcano's crater was used for secret royal burials and for the site of sacrifices of people who broke sacred laws.

The first U.S. civilian to be buried in the Punchbowl when it opened in 1949 was journalist Ernie Pyle, a war correspondent for Scripps-Howard. He lived with and wrote about the soldiers in North Africa, in the campaigns in Italy, in the D-Day invasion of France and on the Pacific Islands. He was killed on one of the islands just four months before the war against Japan ended.[2] Other well-known persons buried here are two astronauts from Hawaii. Astronaut Ellison Onizuka died when the space shuttle *Challenger* exploded shortly after takeoff in 1986. The second astronaut from Hawaii was Charles L. Veach. U.S. Senator Spark Matsunaga's body is also interred in the Punchbowl National Cemetery.

The memorial, built to honor those who died during World War II, is set against one slope of the crater. Approaching the memorial is a long flight of stairs on each side of which are 10 "Courts of the Missing." On the walls of the courts are listed the names of 26,280 U.S. servicemen who were Missing in Action or buried at sea. The names are divided into separate branches of the military and are alphabetized so that people searching for the names of relatives can find them more easily. On the weekends, there are also veterans available to help people find specific names. In front of the staircase is a stone with the following inscription to the Unknown Soldiers: "In these gardens are recorded the names of Americans who gave their lives in the service of their country and whose earthly resting place is known only to God."

At the top of the stairs is a forecourt that is dedicated to all branches of the U.S. military service. The centerpiece of the memorial is a large tower on the front of which is sculpted a large female figure called "Columbia." *Columbia* stands for America, which was discovered by Columbus. The figure is 30 feet tall and holds a laurel branch, the symbol for victory. She stands on a ledge that is in the shape of the prow of a ship. Inside the tower is the chapel. On each side of the chapel are the map galleries, which show battles in the Pacific campaign during World War II. The plants surrounding the memorial and throughout the Punchbowl are either native to Hawaii or imported from various Pacific islands on which U.S. servicemen fought during the war.

---

[1]"Punchbowl National Cemetery":
  http://www.hawaii.edu/~turner/oahu/pnchbwl.htm by Jerry Bourn, Tassa Torres and Rose Bega.
[2]*The Family Encyclopedia of American History*, Pleasantville, New York, The Reader's Digest Association, Inc., 1975.

Punchbowl National Cemetery, Hawaii Questions

1. Why is the cemetery on Pouwaina in Hawaii called the Punchbowl?

   _____

   _____

2. Thought Question: Why is it appropriate that Pouwaina—which means "Hill of Sacrifice"—was

   chosen as one of the national cemeteries? _____

   _____

3. Soldiers from what three U.S. wars are honored at the Punchbowl?_____

   _____

4. Name two nationally famous people buried at the Punchbowl. _____

   _____

5. Using the written description in the last two paragraphs of the text on page 26, draw a view of the memorial as you would see it looking down from the air.

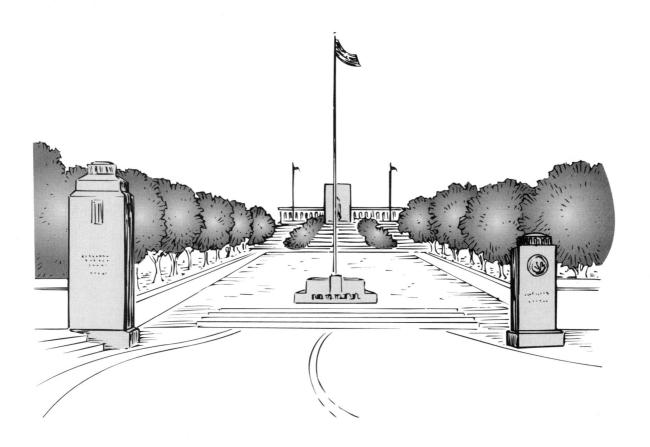

Vietnam War Time Line[1]

1930

Ho Chi Minh organizes the Indochinese Communist Party, which opposes French control of Indochina.

1940

Japanese soldiers invade French Indochina.

1945

August—Japan surrenders to the Allies.

August—Ho Chi Minh creates the Viet Minh, which is a guerrilla army to fight against the French.

September—Vietnam is divided into North Vietnam and South Vietnam.

1946

November—Ho Chi Minh tries to get France to grant independence for Vietnam.

December—France and Vietnam are involved in open warfare.

1950

The United States begins to send economic aid to the French to fight against the Vietnamese.

China, now a Communist nation, supplies the Vietnamese with weapons.

August—The United States sends 35 men to Vietnam as part of the U.S. Military Assistance Advisory Group to aid the French.

1954

May 7—Viet Minh General Vo Nguyen Giap defeats the French forces at Dien Bien Phu. The French-Indochina War has ended, and France leaves Vietnam.

June—The U.S. sends members of the CIA to Saigon, South Vietnam.

June 20—The Geneva Conference on Indochina declares the 17th parallel to be the dividing line between Communist North Vietnam and democratic South Vietnam.

October 24—U.S. President Eisenhower promises to support the South Vietnamese government.

1956

North Vietnam and South Vietnam begin fighting against each other.

---

[1]"Vietnam Yesterday & Today Chronology of U.S. Vietnam Relations, Timeline": servcc.oakton.edu/~wittman/chronol.html

Vietnam War Time Line

1959

July 8—Two U.S. soldiers become the first Americans killed in combat when the Viet Cong (Communist guerrilla army) attack Bien Hoa.

1960

The Communists in South Vietnam organize the Viet Cong, also known as the National Liberation Front (NLF).

1961

February—President Kennedy sends military advisors to South Vietnam. He declares that the troops will fight back if the enemy fires on them.

1963

May-August—Many Buddhists demonstrate against Ngo Dinh Diem's government in South Vietnam for not allowing religious freedom. Some monks commit suicide as part of the protests.

November 1—Ngo Dinh Diem is assassinated in an uprising to overthrow his government.

November 22—Lee Harvey Oswald assassinates President Kennedy in Dallas, Texas.

1964

June 20—General William Westmoreland heads U.S. forces in South Vietnam.

August 2—North Vietnamese torpedo boats attack the U.S. destroyer ship *Maddox* in the Gulf of Tonkin.

August 4—A second alleged North Vietnamese attack, this time against the U.S.S. *Turner Joy*, completes the events that have become known as the Gulf of Tonkin Incident.

August 5—President Johnson calls upon Congress for a resolution against North Vietnam for the attacks on U.S. ships.

August 7—Congress passes the Gulf of Tonkin Resolution that allows the U.S. to respond to further North Vietnamese attacks and to give military aid to members of the Southeast Asia Treaty Organization. (South Vietnam is a member of SEATO.) (Note: Congress never declared war in Vietnam. The Gulf of Tonkin Resolution was the closest the U.S. came to a declaration of war.)

[2]*The American Pageant* (7th ed.) by Thomas A. Bailey and David M. Kennedy, Lexington, Massachusetts, D.C. Heath and Company, 1983.

Vietnam War Time Line

1965

March 8-9—The first U.S. combat troops arrive in South Vietnam.

April 17—The Students for a Democratic Society (SDS) organize an anti-war rally in Washington, D.C.

June—South Vietnamese Generals Nguyen Cao Ky and Nguyen Van Thieu take over the government of their country.

October 15-16—Forty U.S. cities see anti-war demonstrations.

November 14-16—The U.S. and North Vietnamese soldiers fight in the first major battle of the war.

1967

September—Nguyen Van Thieu becomes president of South Vietnam.

October 21-23—Washington, D.C., is the site of an anti-war demonstration by 50,000 people.

1968

January 21-July—The battle of Khe Sanh occurs; North Vietnamese surround U.S. troops.

January 31—The Tet Offensive begins. The Viet Cong attack Hue and the capitals of 31 provinces. The VC even invade the U.S. embassy in Saigon. The U.S. eventually defeats the VC, but the Tet Offensive is a huge shock to U.S. morale.

March 16—U.S. soldiers kill 150 or more Vietnamese civilians in cold blood at My Lai. This event does not become public knowledge until 1969.

March 22—General Creighton W. Abrams replaces William Westmoreland as head of troops in South Vietnam.

May 10—The U.S. and North Vietnam begin the Paris peace talks.

1969

June 8—President Nixon says that he will bring home 25,000 U.S. troops from Vietnam. He plans to return the entire 540,000 Americans gradually. His plan is to "Vietnamize" the Vietnam War, turning most of the fighting over to South Vietnamese soldiers rather than U.S. troops.[2]

September 3—Revolutionary leader Ho Chi Minh dies.

November 15—An anti-war demonstration in Washington, D.C., draws 250,000 participants.

Vietnam War Time Line

1970

April 30—President Nixon sends U.S. and South Vietnamese troops to invade Cambodian sites where the Viet Cong store supplies and hide from attack. This event is seen as a widening of the war instead of the withdrawal that Nixon had promised.

May—National Guardsmen fire on student protesters at Kent State University in Ohio, killing four. Days later, the highway patrol kills two African American students at Jackson State in Mississippi.

1971

U.S. and South Vietnamese troops try to cut off the Ho Chi Minh Trail (a source of supplies from North Vietnam for the Viet Cong) by invading Laos.

1972

December 18—U.S. begins bombing Hanoi (capital of North Vietnam) and other North Vietnamese cities hoping to force the Communists into making progress at the peace conference.

December 28—North Vietnamese agree to return to the peace conference if the U.S. will stop the bombing.

1973

January 23—The United States, South Vietnam and North Vietnam sign the Paris Peace Accords that end the U.S. involvement in the fighting in Vietnam.

January 28—The cease-fire begins as agreed upon in the Paris Peace Accords.

February 12-27—United States prisoners of war begin to return home. (Note: The issue of the recovery of prisoners of war and those missing in action who have been unaccounted for continues into the 21st century.)

March 29—The last U.S. soldiers leave South Vietnam.

1975

April 29-30—North Vietnamese troops invading South Vietnam reach Saigon, the capital city.

The South Vietnamese president surrenders, which ends the Vietnam War.

The U.S. removes the last of its people in Saigon.

The North Vietnamese unite North and South Vietnam in the Independent Socialist Republic of Vietnam.

Vietnam War Time Line Activity

Fill in the events from the time line under the appropriate headings on the outline below. The number of sub-headings for each subject shows how many facts belong under that topic. Choose the most important facts to include under each heading.

I. Ho Chi Minh and his followers rebel against French ownership of Indochina.

    A. _____

    B. _____

    C. _____

    D. _____

II. The United States gradually becomes involved in the war between the Viet Minh and the French.

    A. _____

    B. _____

III. The U.S. increases its commitment to South Vietnam after the French leave.

    A. _____

    B. _____

    C. _____

    D. _____

IV. The Gulf of Tonkin Incident begins open warfare between the U.S. and the North Vietnamese.

    A. _____

    B. _____

    C. _____

    D. _____

    E. _____

V. Demonstrations in the U.S. show the growing feelings against the Vietnam War.

    A. _____

    B. _____

    C. _____

    D. _____

    E. _____

VI. The United States begins peace talks and gradual withdrawal of its troops from Vietnam.

    A. _____

    B. _____

    C. _____

    D. _____

    E. _____

    F. _____

Vietnam POWs & MIAs

Two of the unresolved issues of the Vietnam War that have continued into the 21st century are the Prisoners of War (POWs) who have not returned to the United States and the Missing in Action (MIAs) who have not been accounted for by the Vietnamese government. There are three points of view on this issue: that of the U.S. government, that of the Vietnamese government and that of the families and friends of the POWs and MIAs. As the United States has slowly resumed diplomatic and trade relations with Vietnam, it has been more willing to accept the Vietnamese account of POWs and MIAs as true. At the same time, Vietnam has been more open to answering questions about these issues and to allowing U.S. citizens into Vietnam to search for missing relatives. Some families and friends of POWs and MIAs as well as some veterans of the Vietnam War contend that there are more servicemen left in Vietnam than the U.S. government admits and that the government hasn't done enough to get those men back home.[1]

After the U.S. and North Vietnam signed the Paris Peace Accords in January 1973, U.S. troops began returning to America. In February of that year, Operation Homecoming saw the return of U.S. POWs, some of whom had been held captive for years. North Vietnam released what were presumed to be the last 591 POWs on April 1, 1973.[2] It was-

n't until nine years later in 1982 that relations between the U.S. and Vietnam[3] warmed enough for the two countries to talk about U.S. men missing in action. Vietnamese officials agreed to talks on the issue of MIAs in 1982 and actively began to participate in joint investigations on the whereabouts of MIAs in 1988. By 1995, the Vietnamese government was willing to provide detailed documents and maps on U.S. MIAs that answered some questions about the missing.[4] By 1999, Vietnam had returned the bodies of 506 U.S. servicemen.[5]

The All POW-MIA organization on its web site claims that, as of 1999, there were at least 43 U.S. servicemen last known to be alive in Vietnam. It also claims that "several hundred men vanished into a black hole" with the U.S. invasion of Cambodia in the spring of 1970 and that neither the Vietnamese nor the Pathet Lao (the Communist ruling party in Laos) has returned any of these men.[6] On the other hand, the federal government claims that, as of November 2001, the governments of Vietnam, China, Laos and Cambodia have returned the remains of 637 POW or MIA servicemen to the U.S. In addition, the government claims that it has looked into 21,794 accounts of sightings of live POW/MIAs and has found only 17 of these reports to be unresolved.[7]

---

[1]"U.S. POW/MIAs in Southeast Asia: In Search of the Truth": www.wtvi.com/wesley/powmia/powpap8.htm
by Wesley Fryer © 1991-2000 (At the end of his paper, Wesley provides an extensive bibliography that students could use for further research on this topic.)

[2]"Chronology of U.S.-Vietnam Relations": http://servercc.oakton.edu/~wittman/chronol.htm

[3]From 1954 to 1975, Vietnam was divided into Communist North Vietnam and democratic South Vietnam. After North Vietnam defeated South Vietnam on April 30, 1975, the two countries were united under Communist rule as the Independent Socialist Republic of Vietnam. That is why some places in the text speak of North Vietnam and others call the country only Vietnam.

[4]"Chronology of U.S.-Vietnam Relations," p. 6.

[5]"Key Dates in Post-War U.S.-Vietnam Relations": www.aiipowmia.com/sea/vndates.htm

[6]All POW-MIA "Last Known Alive (LKA) Cases Vietnam Only—As of 1999": www.aiipowmia.com/sea/lka.htm

[7]"Subject: Vietnam Era Unaccounted for Statistical Report, Current as of: November 7, 2001":
http://lcweb2.loc.gov/frd/pow/Nov0701.htm

Vietnam POWs & MIAs Questions

1. Name the three groups or governments that have different opinions on the POW/MIA issue.

   _____

   _____

2. What is the best piece of information in the text to support the idea that Vietnam has been cooperative in returning the remains of MIAs?_____

   _____

   _____

3. What is the best piece of information in the text to support the idea that the U.S. government has done all it can to search for POWs and MIAs?_____

   _____

   _____

4. What are two quotations or statistics that support the claim of POW/MIA families that there are still missing servicemen in Vietnam or Cambodia? _____

   _____

   _____

5. a. Which of the sources on POW/MIAs gives the most recent information on the subject? b. Why is the date of a source important in weighing evidence? _____

   _____

   _____

6. Based on information in this article, do you think that there are still POWs and MIAs left in Vietnam, Cambodia or Laos? On the back of this sheet, write a paragraph explaining your point of view. Use information from the article to support your answer.

Internet Research Ideas

Tomb of the Unknowns & Arlington National Cemetery

1. Research and report on Robert E. Lee's career as a general during the Civil War.

2. Use the web site on Arlington National Cemetery to find the names of African American Congressional Medal of Honor winners buried there. Research several of these men to find out about their lives and the deeds that won them their country's highest medal.

3. What is the history of the quarry at Marble, Colorado, that provided the stone for the Tomb of the Unknowns?

4. Who designed and sculpted the Tomb of the Unknowns? What was his life story?

World War I

5. What was it like to live in and fight from the trenches on the Western Front in France?

6. Report on the development and use of one of the following weapons that were used for the first time in warfare during World War I: a. machine guns, b. tanks, c. airplanes and d. submarines.

7. Report on the wartime career of T.E. Lawrence ("Lawrence of Arabia") who helped the Arabs fight for their independence from the Turks. To what extent were his efforts successful during the war and during the peace conference that followed the war?

8. Research the Russian Revolution of 1917. a. Report on Germany's plan to send V.I. Lenin from Switzerland into Russia in a sealed boxcar so that he would start a second, Communist revolution and take Russia out of the fighting against Germany. b. Find out how Lenin started and won the "October Revolution" that brought the Communists to power in Russia.

9. What did Sergeant Alvin C. York do during World War I to become the most famous U.S. soldier of that war? How did fame change his life from the way it had been before the war?

10. Research and report on General John "Black Jack" Pershing's career as the leader of the American Expeditionary Forces during World War I.

11. Before General Pershing led the American Expeditionary Forces into battle in World War I, he chased Pancho Villa around Mexico. Villa had invaded the United States and killed 19 people at Columbus, New Mexico, in March 1916. Research and report on this interesting incident in U.S. history. Did Pershing ever catch and punish Villa?

12. There was a strong pacifist movement in the U.S. during World War I. One of the leaders of this movement, Jane Addams, won the Nobel Peace Prize for her work. a. Research Ms. Addams' work in the peace movement both during and after World War I, including her involvement with the Women's Peace Party and the Women's International League for Peace and Freedom. b. Find out about her work at Hull House with the poor and immigrants in Chicago from 1889 onward.

13. The Lafayette Escadrille was a unit of U.S. pilots who fought in World War I on the side of the Allies (Britain, France and Russia) before the United States entered the war in 1917. Among the interesting things about this unit is that it included at least one African American pilot, who was no longer allowed to fly when the U.S. entered the war and took over the squadron.

14. The sinking of the British ship *Lusitania* was controversial not only because of the number of civilians who lost their lives but because of the rumor that the passenger ship was carrying ammunition to Britain for the war effort. Find out what happened to the *Lusitania* and the truth or falsity of the accusations about carrying munitions.

World War II

15. Why were Japanese-Americans who lived on the West Coast of the United States taken from their homes and moved into internment camps in the interior of the country during World War II? What were their lives like in the camps?

16. Several Japanese-Americans who fought in World War II are buried in Arlington National Cemetery. Research and report on the 442 Japanese-American unit that fought in Italy with great distinction during the war.

17. The following are some famous U.S. generals and their major campaigns. Choose one general and report on his career during the war. a. Dwight D. Eisenhower and the D-Day invasion of France; b. Douglas MacArthur and the battles for the Philippines both before he was driven out and on his re-conquest of the islands; c. Mark Clark in Italy; d. "Vinegar Joe" Stillwell and the Burma/Ledo Road in Burma; e. George S. Patton and his tank corps in Europe, especially his rescue of the besieged Bastogne during the Battle of the Bulge; f. Omar Bradley in North Africa and Europe; g. Jonathan Wainwright and the battle for Corregidor in the Philippines.

18. The United Nations is an outgrowth of World War II and the cooperation among the Allied Powers during the war. Find out how the U.N. was founded through conferences such as those at Dunbarton Oaks and San Francisco in 1945-1946.

19. Eleanor Roosevelt was one of the most influential and controversial First Ladies to ever serve in the White House. Because FDR was crippled by polio, Eleanor became his "eyes and ears" and traveled around the country to collect information for him. After her husband's death, Eleanor became a delegate to the United Nations from 1945-1952. Research and report on this woman's extraordinary life.

20. Research any of the battles or other events on the "World War II Time Line" on pages 16-18.

Post-World War II United States

21. Douglas MacArthur was Supreme Commander of Allied Powers in occupied Japan after World War II. Report on MacArthur's career as the head of the occupying forces, his involvement in the new Japanese constitution and his influence on Japanese history and culture.

22. One of the great achievements of the U.S. after World War II was the Marshall Plan to rebuild Europe after the destruction the war caused there. Research and report on Secretary of State George C. Marshall, his Marshall Plan and the success of the plan in post-war Europe.

23. In December 1947, Jackie Robinson became the first African American to play in major league baseball when Branch Rickey signed him up as a Brooklyn Dodger. (The Dodgers played in Brooklyn before they moved to Los Angeles.) Find out about Robinson's career in the major leagues, the discrimination he experienced as an African American player and his influence on the further integration of baseball.

Korean War

24. General Douglas MacArthur's amphibious landing at Inchon, Korea, was an incredible feat. Research and report on his plan, how it was carried out and the immediate effect it had on the Korean War.

25. How were Douglas MacArthur, Charley McCarthy and Joseph McCarthy—all well-known figures in the early 1950s—different from each other? To show differences, you must tell who all three figures were. Write one or two sentences about each of the three; then go on to give the most information about Charley McCarthy's career.

26. After World War II, President Truman ordered the integration of the armed forces so that African Americans would now fight alongside white Americans. a. Investigate and report on Truman's orders for integration, what prompted him to do this and the immediate reaction and results among white and African American troops. b. Research the effect that integration had on the troops and fighting in the Korean War.

27. The Korean War period was also the era of McCarthyism. Senator Joseph McCarthy made accusations that there were Communists in the State Department of the federal government. Soon, the U.S. was deep in a "witch hunt" for Communists in the government, colleges, the movie industry and the Army. Research and report on McCarthyism and the rise and fall of Senator Joseph McCarthy.

28. Explain how Korea became divided along the 38th parallel between Communist North Korea and democratic South Korea after World War II. How did the elections in South Korea in 1948 worsen relations between North and South Korea? In general, what was the political history of Korea between 1945 and 1950 that led to the Korean War?

29. The Soviet Union developed its own atomic bomb in 1949 only four years after the U.S. invented the bomb. In 1951, Ethel and Julius Rosenberg were tried in the United States for passing atomic secrets to the Soviet Union. Although the Rosenbergs protested their innocence, they were both executed in June 1953. Research the Rosenbergs' case and report on it to your classmates. Include in your report your own conclusions about the Rosenbergs' guilt or innocence.

Vietnam War Era

30. Henry Kissinger of the U.S. and Le Duc Tho of North Vietnam won the Nobel Peace Prize for ending U.S. fighting in Vietnam. Investigate and report on the lives of these two men and their work together to end the war between their two nations.

31. What really happened in the Gulf of Tonkin on August 2 and 4, 1964? Research current information about these two incidents and report your findings. In your opinion, was the war in Vietnam justified based on what happened in the Gulf of Tonkin?

32. Research any of the battles or major events on the "Vietnam War Time Line" on pages 28-31.

33. In November 1963, South Vietnamese generals overthrew the government of President Ngo Dinh Diem and assassinated him and his brother. Find out about this event, its cause and the extent to which the U.S. was behind the overthrow of the government through the CIA or other agency.

34. In October 1964, the Reverend Martin Luther King, Jr., received the Nobel Peace Prize for his work on civil rights for African Americans in the United States. Find out about Dr. King's civil rights work and his assassination in April 1968.

35. Cassius Marcellus Clay (who later changed his name to Muhammad Ali) defeated Sonny Liston in February 1964 to win the World Heavyweight Championship in boxing. Later, Ali protested against being drafted to fight in the Vietnam War on religious grounds as a Muslim. He was stripped of his title and not allowed to fight. Research Muhammad Ali, his career as one of the greatest boxers of all time and his protest against the Vietnam War.

Multiple Intelligence Activities

Verbal/Linguistic Intelligence

1. World War I produced several soldier-poets including Wilfred Owen, Siegfried Sassoon, Rupert Brooke and Joyce Kilmer. Owen and Sassoon were known for their powerful anti-war poetry, while Brooke and Kilmer wrote on more general topics. Using the works of these and other poets of the World War I era, create an oral interpretation presentation on a specific theme that you can perform for your classmates.

2. Do historical research on the controversy between President Truman and General MacArthur during the Korean War. a. If only two to four students are interested in this topic, they could debate whether or not MacArthur should have been fired. b. If many students are interested, they could conduct a court marshal of MacArthur. Students not directly involved as one of the participants in the trial could serve as the jury.

Visual/Spatial Intelligence

1. Go on the internet to the web site for the American Battle Monuments Commission. This group supervises the monuments and cemeteries of U.S. servicemen killed overseas. All of these cemeteries have unknown soldiers buried in them. Download pictures of the monuments from these cemeteries and make a collage or a PowerPoint presentation that you can show to your class.

2. Research monuments designed for World War I, World War II, the Korean War and the Vietnam War. After viewing the variety of memorials that have been designed, create a memorial to those Americans who died in the Persian Gulf War in 1991. You can either draw your design or build a model of it.

3. *All Quiet on the Western Front* is a famous anti-war novel written by a German author after World War I. At least two versions of the movie with the same name as the book were filmed. Watch the movie and make a list of the anti-war images the author and the film's director used. After watching the movie, sketch two or three of the images that you think made the strongest anti-war statement.

Auditory/Musical Intelligence

1. Compose a serious piece of music in honor of the Tomb of the Unknown Soldier. It can be in any musical form. One possibility is to compose a song and write patriotic lyrics to go with it.

2. Research songs from the different eras mentioned in this book. Select several pieces that you like and sing or play them for your class. The following are some of the types of music you can choose from: a. patriotic World War I songs; b. patriotic World War II songs; c. big band and swing music from the 1940s; d. jazz as it developed in the 1950s and 1960s; e. Vietnam anti-war songs.

Multiple Intelligence Activities

Logical/Mathematical Intelligence

1. Research World War I, World War II, the Korean War and the Vietnam War. Then make a chart showing the number of soldiers killed, the number wounded, the number missing in action, the length of U.S. involvement in each war and the total cost of the war.

2. Play a board game based on World War I or II. Two very good games are Diplomacy about World War I and Axis and Allies about World War II. The games should be based on strategy and logic, not on luck and dice.

Bodily/Kinesthetic Intelligence

1. Research the type of training that Navy SEALS endure in order to become members of that special fighting force. What mental and physical tests do they have to pass to be able to join the SEALS? Under adult supervision, test yourself on a modified version of the physical tasks the SEALS have to complete.

2. Have students research a specific war; create brief scenes of some of the most important events from that war; and act out the scenes in chronological order. For example, if the students did scenes from World War II, they might present the bombing of Pearl Harbor, the D-Day invasion of Normandy, MacArthur's return to the Philippines, the raising of the U.S. flag on the mountain in Iwo Jima and the Japanese signing of the terms of surrender on the U.S.S. *Missouri*.

Interpersonal Intelligence

1. U.S. General Dwight D. Eisenhower, British General Bernard Montgomery and German General Erwin Rommel all had different styles of leadership and used different tactics to win battles. Research each of the three generals and write a report on what qualities of leadership, intelligence and personality made each of these men successful leaders even though they were so different from one another.

2. Before World War II began with the invasion of Poland in 1939, Britain and France gave in to Hitler's demands for land (or didn't stop him when he took over land) at least four times. Research these land grabs in 1938-1939, especially the Munich Conference in September 1938. Pretend you are the Prime Minister of Britain. How would you resolve Hitler's demands without starting a war and without betraying Czechoslovakia to the Germans? Write out your plans for conflict resolution.

Multiple Intelligence Activities

Intrapersonal Intelligence

1. Were any of your relatives involved in World War I, World War II, the Korean War or the Vietnam War? They might have been soldiers, nurses, conscientious objectors who served the U.S. in other ways or active in an anti-war movement. If your family is willing to discuss these relatives and/or still have their personal papers, you could do a family history. Possibilities include recorded oral stories about family members, a scrapbook of copies of photographs and documents, or a history compiled and written by the student.

2. Research to find a famous photograph from one of the wars. Some examples would be the desolate Western Front from World War I, a concentration camp survivor from World War II, the retreat of the Marines from Chosen Reservoir in Korea or the people trying to leave Saigon by helicopter from the U.S. embassy at the end of the Vietnam War. Pretend that you are one of the figures in the photograph and write at least two pages describing in the first person what happened to you in that situation.

Multiple Intelligence

Write a play about the two men who were chosen in 1958 to represent World War II and the Korean War at the Tomb of the Unknowns. The play should be about the way they were chosen to be the Unknowns, how they were transported to the U.S. and the ceremonies performed at their burial. It is possible to give the two Unknowns parts in the play so that they occasionally comment on what is happening to them and their memories of their wars. People of all the intelligences will have roles in this project including writing, directing, building scenery, designing costumes, overseeing the budget, acting and creating advertisements on a computer.

Answer Key

Tomb of the Unknowns Questions, page 7

1. The Tomb of the Unknowns was originally built to honor a soldier from World War I.

2. For each war, a Medal of Honor winner chose the Unknown Soldier. Four caskets of unknown soldiers who died in the war were dug up and brought together. The Congressional Medal of Honor winner chose among the four caskets. The person chosen at random was then buried in the Tomb of the Unknowns.

3. The President of the U.S. is also Commander in Chief of the armed forces. That title is what makes it appropriate for him to preside over a military burial at the Tomb of the Unknowns.

4. Two soldiers were chosen in 1958 because one was to honor those who died in World War II, and the other honored the dead from the Korean War.

5. No Unknown Soldier from the Vietnam War is buried at the Tomb of the Unknowns because the remains of the soldier who was buried there have been identified as 1st Lt. Blassie. He is, therefore, no longer unknown. It is likely that DNA testing would identify any other person from the Vietnam War as well, so there is no one to bury as an Unknown from that era.

6. Answers will vary. Give credit for answers with logical supporting arguments.

Arlington National Cemetery Questions, page 9

1.

George Washington + Martha Custis Washington

George Washington Parke Custis

Mary Anna Randolph Custis Lee + Robert E. Lee

2. a. The federal government first gained custody of Arlington when it confiscated it from Mary Anna Randolph Lee because she did not pay the property taxes in person. Then a tax commissioner bought the land at a public auction.
b. In 1883, the federal government bought the land for $150,000 from George Washington Custis Lee.

3. Famous groups of people buried at Arlington National Cemetery include 1800 men who were killed at Bull Run, veterans of the American Revolution, World War II veterans, men who fought in the Persian Gulf War, three Chief Justices and eight Associate Justices of the Supreme Court, African American Congressional Medal of Honor winners, Japanese-American servicemen from World War II, several astronauts and important women in U.S. history.

4. The three Unknowns buried at the Tomb of the Unknowns gave their lives for the United States. They also represent all of those men who died in World War I, World War II and the Korean War. That is why it is appropriate that the sentinels at the Tomb be of the highest physical and mental caliber.

5. Most of the U.S. Presidents are not buried at Arlington because they or their families wanted them to be buried in their hometowns.

World War I Questions, page 12

1. The immediate cause of World War I was the assassination of Archduke Francis Ferdinand.

2. Austria-Hungary opposed Serbia because of the assassination of the Archduke. Russia supported its fellow Slavs in Serbia, which meant it opposed Austria-Hungary. Germany gave its unconditional support to Austria-Hungary because they were both members of the Triple Alliance. (Italy, likewise, supported Germany and Austria-Hungary because of the Triple Alliance.) France sided with Russia against Germany because of the Triple Entente. When Germany invaded Belgium and France, Great Britain was drawn into the war because of its membership in the Triple Entente. Therefore, because of the system of alliances in Europe before World War I, six major nations on that continent were immediately drawn into the fighting.

Answer Key

3. **Allied Powers in 1914**
France
Russia
Great Britain

Allied Powers in 1918
France
Great Britain
Japan
Italy
United States

Central Powers in 1914
Germany
Austria-Hungary
Italy

Central Powers in 1918
Germany
Austria-Hungary
Bulgaria
Turkey

4. a. The U.S. was eventually drawn into World War I on the side of the Allies because of Germany's practice of unrestricted submarine warfare. b. A specific example of this submarine warfare was Germany's torpedoing of the *Lusitania* with the loss of 1198 lives, including 128 Americans.

5. It took about seven months for the U.S. to train its soldiers, transport them to Europe and become actively engaged in the fighting there.

6. U.S. troops fought in France at Ypres, Cantigny, Soissons, Belleau Wood, Chateau-Thierry, the Meuse-Argonne and St. Mihiel.

7. The U.S. troops at Belleau Wood and Chateau-Thierry helped the French stop the last major German offensive against Paris, the capital of France.

8. November 11, 1918, was the day the fighting stopped at the end of World War I. For 35 years thereafter, November 11 was celebrated in the U.S. as Armistice Day. In 1954, Congress made November 11 Veterans Day so that the soldiers of World War II and the Korean War would officially be honored on that day along with the veterans of World War I.

General Pershing & the World War I Monuments Questions, page 15

1. Pershing wanted to limit the size and number of U.S. monuments in France because he didn't want to offend the French. The U.S. had lost 80,000 men in the fighting as compared to France's loss of 1,000,000 men. It would be offensive for the U.S. monuments to outshine those of the French.

2. New cemeteries were needed after World War I ended for two reasons. First, the cemeteries created during the war were in inconvenient places for the farmers who were trying to restore their fields and plant crops. Second, the wartime cemeteries were run down and there were no provisions for upkeep.

3. a. The ABMC built five minor cemeteries and monuments. b. The three major monuments were built at Chateau-Thierry, Montsec and Montfaucon.

4. There were at least two reasons why tourists would want to visit monuments and cemeteries from old wars. First, they might be looking for the graves of ancestors or the listing of their names on the memorials to those missing in action. Second, they might be interested in history or have a sense of the importance of great battles and wars that happened in the past. They might also have a sense of the importance of those wars to our nation's survival and prosperity today.

World War II Time Line Activities, page 19

1. A. German Aggression:
   September 1, 1939—Germany invades Poland
   April 9, 1940—German troops invade Denmark and Norway
   May 10, 1940—German troops invade Netherlands, Luxemburg, Belgium and France
   July-October 1940—German submarines sink 217 merchant ships in the Atlantic
   September 7, 1940—Germans begin air raids on London, England (the Blitz)
   April 6, 1941—Germany invades Yugoslavia and Greece
   June 22, 1941—Germany attacks Soviet Union
   August 20, 1941—beginning of German siege of Leningrad in the Soviet Union
   B. Italian Aggression:
   July 4, 1940—Italian troops attack the Sudan
   August 4-21, 1940—Italians occupy British Somaliland
   September 11, 1940—Italian troops attack Egypt
   October 28, 1940—Italian troops invade Greece
   March 9, 1941—Italians attack Albania, but invasion fails

Answer Key

C. Japanese Aggression:

September 22, 1940—Japanese troops invade northern French Indochina

December 7, 1941—Japanese ships and planes attack Pearl Harbor, Hawaii

December 7-8, 1941—Japanese invade Malaya, Hong Kong, Guam, Midway, Wake, the Philippine Islands and Thailand

December 16, 1941—Japanese invade Borneo and Burma

D. Soviet Aggression:

September 17, 1939—Soviet Union invades Poland from the east

November 30, 1939—Soviet troops invade Finland

July 25, 1940—Soviet Union annexes Latvia, Estonia and Lithuania

2. These are the events that show the turning points during 1942 as the Allies begin to win the war.

March 14—U.S. troops arrive in Australia to begin Pacific counteroffensive

April 18—Doolittle leads U.S. bombers in first attack on Tokyo, Japan

May 4-8—Allies win Battle of the Coral Sea in the Pacific Ocean

June 4-8—Allies defeat Japanese in Battle of Midway in Pacific Ocean

August 7—U.S. troops land on Guadalcanal in the Solomon Islands

November 8—U.S. and other Allied troops land in Morocco and Algeria

November 11—last German and Italian troops driven out of Egypt

November 12-15—Allies win naval Battle of Guadalcanal

3. A. Europe

January 27—first U.S. air raids on Germany

February 2—last German troops surrender in Stalingrad, Soviet Union

July 9-10—U.S. troops invade Sicily, an island that is part of Italy

September 3—Italians secretly surrender to the United States, but German troops continue to fight against Allies in Italy

September 9—Allied troops land at Salerno, Italy

B. Asian Mainland

November 28-30—Big Three meet at Teheran (Iran) Conference. (Iran is in the Middle East, which is part of the Asian mainland.)

C. Pacific Ocean and its Islands

June 29-30—Australian and U.S. troops land in New Guinea

November 20-23—U.S. troops capture Tarawa in Gilbert Islands

D. North Africa

February 14-25—Germans defeat Allies at Battle of Kasserine Pass, Tunisia

May 13—Axis troops (German and Italian) surrender in North Africa

4. The Allies captured Italy ("captured Rome") and France ("captured Paris").

5. a. Below are several events that show that the Soviet Union was fighting on the side of the Allies in 1945. Students only need two correct answers for this question.

April 25—U.S. and Soviet troops meet at Torgau, Germany, on the Elbe River

May 2—Germans surrender Italy to Allies; Berlin, Germany, surrenders to Soviets

May 8—V.E. Day (Victory in Europe); Germans surrender to Soviet Union

August 8—Soviet Union declares war against Japan

b. These two events in 1941 explain why the Soviet Union switched sides and supported the Allies.

June 22—Germany attacks Soviet Union

August 20—beginning of German siege of Leningrad in the Soviet Union

Answer Key

International World War II Cemeteries Chart, page 22

Questions	North Africa American Cemetery & Memorial	Manila American Cemetery & Memorial	Florence American Cemetery & Memorial	Normandy American Cemetery & Memorial
Continent Where Located	Africa	Asia (Pacific Islands)	Europe	Europe
Located Near What City or Site	Carthage, Tunisia	Manila, Philippines	Florence, Italy	Omaha Beach in France
Number of U.S. Dead Buried at the Cemetery	2841	17,206	4402	9386
Number of Missing in Action Listed at Cemetery	3724	36,282	1409	1557
Size of Cemetery (in acres)	27	152	70	172
Describe the Major Military Action Associated with the Cemetery	The major action was the invasion of North Africa to defeat Germany and Italy.	The cemetery honors those who fought in the Pacific, especially in the Philippines and in New Guinea.	The major action was the invasion in Italy against the Axis Powers.	The major operation was the D-Day invasion of Normandy in France.

Memorial Includes Which of the Following?

Chapel	Yes	Yes	Yes	Yes
Maps of Operation	Yes	No. (There are maps, but that information is not in the text.)	Yes	Yes
Names of Missing Men	Yes	Yes	Yes	Yes
Statues	No	No	Yes	Yes
Column/Pillar	No	No	Yes	No

Answer Key

Korean War Questions, page 25

1. The Korean War began when North Korean troops crossed the 38th parallel to invade South Korea.

2. General MacArthur bypassed the battle lines at the southern end of the Korean peninsula to make an amphibious landing at Inchon, which is near the 38th parallel and Seoul, the capital of South Korea.

3. The U.S. did not want to draw China or the Soviet Union into the Korean War.

4. a. Truman fired MacArthur because the general was insubordinate. The President, as Commander in Chief of the military, gave MacArthur specific orders; but the general kept criticizing his leader publicly. b. Answers will vary. Give credit for answers that use historical facts and logic.

5. Probably a major reason the Korean War became "the forgotten war" was that there was no clear victory for the U.S. in the war. The boundary line between North and South Korea ended up at exactly the same place it was before the war began. People tend to forget what they view as their "failures."

6. The Soviet Union, the United States, France, Great Britain and China are permanent members of the United Nations Security Council because they were the Allies (with the exception of Communist China) who won World War II. As permanent members, they have the veto power. A veto by any one of those five nations will stop any proposal that comes before the Security Council.

Punchbowl National Cemetery, Hawaii Questions, page 27

1. The cemetery is called the Punchbowl because it lies in the crater of an extinct volcano that is shaped like a bowl.

2. It is appropriate that the cemetery be on the volcano called "Hill of Sacrifice" because U.S. servicemen in the cemetery gave their lives for their country.

3. Soldiers from World War II, the Korean War and the Vietnam War are honored at the Punchbowl National Cemetery.

4. Two people who are nationally famous who are buried in the Punchbowl National Cemetery are Ernie Pyle, World War II journalist; and astronaut Ellison Onizuka, who died in the *Challenger* explosion in 1986.

5.

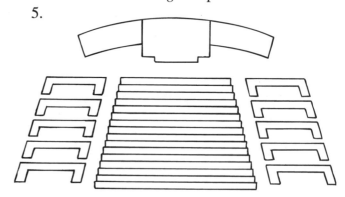

Answer Key

Vietnam War Time Line Activity, page 32

I. Ho Chi Minh and his followers rebel against French ownership of Indochina.
   A. 1930—Ho Chi Minh organizes the Indochinese Communist Party, which opposes French control of Indochina.
   B. August 1945—Ho Chi Minh creates the Viet Minh, which is a guerrilla army to fight against the French.
   C. November 1946—Ho Chi Minh tries to get France to grant independence for Vietnam.
   D. December 1946—France and Vietnam are involved in open warfare.

II. The United States gradually becomes involved in the war between the Viet Minh and the French.
   A. 1950—The United States begins to send economic aid to the French to fight against the Vietnamese.
   B. August 1950—The United States sends 35 men to Vietnam as part of the U.S. Military Assistance Advisory Group to aid the French.

III. The U.S. increases its commitment to South Vietnam after the French leave.
   A. June 1954—The U.S. sends members of the CIA to Saigon, South Vietnam.
   B. October 24, 1954—U.S. President Eisenhower promises to support the South Vietnamese government.
   C. July 8, 1959—Two U.S. soldiers become the first Americans killed in combat when the Viet Cong attack Bien Hoa.
   D. February 1961—President Kennedy sends military advisors to South Vietnam. He declares that the troops will fight back if the enemy fires on them.

IV. The Gulf of Tonkin Incident begins open warfare between the U.S. and the North Vietnamese.
   A. August 2, 1964—North Vietnamese torpedo boats attack the U.S. destroyer ship *Maddox* in the Gulf of Tonkin.
   B. August 4, 1964—A second alleged North Vietnamese attack, this time against the U.S.S. *Turner Joy*, completes the events that have become known as the Gulf of Tonkin Incident.
   C. August 5, 1964—President Johnson calls upon Congress for a resolution against North Vietnam for the attacks on U.S. ships.
   D. August 7, 1964—Congress passes the Gulf of Tonkin Resolution that allows the U.S. to respond to further North Vietnamese attacks and to give military aid to members of the Southeast Asia Treaty Organization.
   E. March 8-9, 1965—The first U.S. combat troops arrive in South Vietnam.

V. Demonstrations in the U.S. show the growing feelings against the Vietnam War.
   A. April 17, 1965—The Students for a Democratic Society organize an anti-war rally in Washington, D.C.
   B. October 15-16, 1965—Forty U.S. cities see anti-war demonstrations.
   C. October 21-23, 1967—Washington, D.C., is the site of an anti-war demonstration by 50,000 people.
   D. November 15, 1969—An anti-war demonstration in Washington, D.C., draws 250,000 participants.
   E. May 1970—National Guardsmen fire on student protesters at Kent State University in Ohio, killing four.

Answer Key

VI. The United States begins peace talks and gradual withdrawal of its troops from Vietnam.
   A. May 10, 1968—The U.S. and North Vietnam begin the Paris peace talks.
   B. June 8, 1969—President Nixon says that he will bring home 25,000 U.S. troops from Vietnam. He plans to return the entire 540,000 Americans gradually.
   C. December 18, 1972—U.S. begins bombing Hanoi and other North Vietnamese cities hoping to force the Communists into making progress at the peace conference.
   D. December 28, 1972—North Vietnamese agree to return to the peace conference if the U.S. will stop the bombing.
   E. January 23, 1973—The United States, South Vietnam and North Vietnam sign the Paris Peace Accords that end the U.S. involvement in the fighting in Vietnam.
   F. January 28, 1973—The cease-fire begins as agreed upon in the Paris Peace Accords.
   G. February 12-27, 1973—United States prisoners of war begin to return home.
   H. March 29, 1973—The last U.S. soldiers leave South Vietnam.
(Note: Students only need six events to complete this last segment of the outline.)

Vietnam POWs & MIAs Questions, page 34
1. The three points of view on the POW/MIA issue are that of the U.S. government, that of the Vietnamese government and those of the families and friends of the POWs and MIAs.
2. The best proof that Vietnam has been cooperative in the MIA investigations is the statement that its government has returned the bodies of 506 servicemen as of 1999.
3. The best proof that the U.S. government has done all it can do in the search for POWs and MIAs is that it has investigated 21,794 reports of sightings of servicemen and has cleared all except 17 of those reports.
4. Two pieces of evidence support the families' claims that there are still POWs and MIAs missing. The first are the 43 last known alive cases still open as of 1999. The second is the quotation that "several hundred men vanished into a black hole" in Laos.
5. a. The *Vietnam Era Unaccounted for Statistical Report* that was published November 7, 2001, is the most recent evidence on the subject of POWs and MIAs. b. The date of evidence is important because the most up-to-date information is likely to be more accurate. For instance, it is possible that more men or bodies have been recovered since the 1999 *Last Known Alive Report* and that it is no longer accurate.
6. Answers will vary. Give credit for paragraphs that use logic and correct historical facts.